Carpaccio

08. APR 99
11 MAY 2002
23 APR 2003
Towcester
23 JAN 2004
13 SEP 2004
-1 AUG 2007
-1 AUG 2007
-3 MAR 2008
-4 Jun 2008.

ZUFFI, S.

Carpaccio

NORTHAMPTONSHIRE
CENTRAL LIBRARY

Please return or renew this item by the last date shown. You may renew items (unless they have been requested by another customer) by telephoning, writing to or calling in at any library.

100% recycled paper

BKS 1 (5/95)

Cover
Two Court Ladies, *detail*
ca. 1490. Venice,
Museo Correr.

Texts by Stefano Zuffi
Translation by Huw Evans

Photograph References
Amoretti, Parma
Electa Archives, Milan
Cameraphoto, Venice
Saporetti, Milan
Scala, Florence
Somaini, Milan
Studio Pizzi, Milan

NORTHAMPTONSHIRE LIBRARIES
AND INFORMATION SERVICES
Askews 8.3.99
759.5 £5.95

Printed in Italy
© 1996 by **Electa**, Milan
Elemond Editori Associati
All Rights Reserved

This volume was printed by Elemond S.p.a.
at the plant in Martellago (Venice) in 1996

Carpaccio

Electa/Art Books International

Carpaccio

Twelve studies for men's heads, drawing.
London, British Museum.

Vittore Carpaccio was an artist who set considerable store by his career: he sought and obtained official appointments, had links with important clients outside Venice, and took part in competitions and public initiatives. He was a man, in other words, of his time, and should not be seen as someone who was nostalgic for the past.

And yet it is hard to resist the temptation of setting Carpaccio apart from the plethora of innovations and proposals that emerged in rapid succession at the turn of the century. While Giovanni Bellini, Giorgione, and Titian were engaged in staging and consolidating the revolution of tonal painting, based on the effects of light on color and concerned with conveying the immediate emotional effects of the atmosphere, Carpaccio hung back, content to be patient. First by means of the most accurate and detailed drawings in the whole tradition of painting in Veneto, and then through his great capacity to see and reproduce the most minute aspects of reality, the artist composed scenes crowded with figures and details, to be savored element by element until the eye forgets the main subject and loses itself in endless vistas.

Carpaccio's paintings possess an indubitable charm, that is obvious to all. On the other hand, a more attentive critical examination cannot fail to reveal the fact that the artist showed little capacity to renew his own style over the course of the years, to enter into dialogue with the more vivid and advanced figurative ideas that emerged in Veneto during the first twenty years of the 16th century. It is a fairly curious fact, as well as a significant one, that the experts find themselves in considerable difficulties when it comes to dating some of Carpaccio's works, with the result that their opinions can differ by more than three decades.

At the slow and constant pace of a gondola slipping through the canals, Carpaccio's painting continues along its own course, bobbing gently through the labyrinth of the soul, a labyrinth made up of faint presences and delicate rays of light. And you cannot tell whether what you are seeing is a real image or a gilded dream, a Venice-Atlantis in which time has truly come to a stop.

From the Mists of His Early Years to the Bright Light of the Legend of Saint Ursula (ca. 1460–1495)

Carpaccio made his official appearance on the Venetian art scene in the year 1490, the date of the first of the canvases he painted for the *Legend of Saint Ursula*. But it seems obvious that, by this time, Carpaccio had already completed his apprenticeship, and indeed was already approaching the peak of his maturity as an artist.

The painter's birth can be dated, on a purely deductive basis, to around 1460–1465, seeing as how by the first known date (1490) Carpaccio appears to be completely mature from the artistic viewpoint. The influences of his youth were undoubtedly the "narrative" painters of the second half of the Quattrocento, and Gentile Bellini in particular. In fact Carpaccio found the ideal dimension for his art in cycles of canvases depicting "scenes" from the life of saints. In this particular genre, typical of Venetian art up until the middle of the Cinquecento, he was indeed unexcelled, in part because he found himself so much at ease with the technique of painting on canvas, still fairly experimental at that time.

In his narrative canvases, despite the fact that the story is skillfully split up into individual scenes that are filled with action and figures, Carpaccio never loses sight of the rigor of a compositional structure based on perspective. In order to have acquired such a sure geometric feeling for space, he must have come into contact with Antonello da Messina, either directly (Antonello was in Venice in 1475–1476) or through the talented go-between of Alvise Vivarini, with whom Carpaccio also shares the way of handling light. In the view of some critics, in addition, it is possible that Carpaccio made a journey to Ancona, which would have given him the opportunity to pass through Urbino and see the paintings of Piero della Francesca. Apropos of journeys, the suggestion has also been made that Carpaccio spent some time in the Middle East (Syria or the Holy Land), in order to explain the abundance of Oriental-style costumes and architecture in his paintings. In reality, very many merchants from different countries passed through Venice, and the variety of their clothing was evident to all. As far as the buildings are concerned, prints, drawings, and book illustrations could have provided plentiful (though not always reliable) information.

In short, it can be concluded that Carpaccio's training and career as an artist took place largely in Venice, and commenced at a very special moment: the moment, that is, when Giovanni Bellini achieved, through a particular use of light, a delicate and highly sensitive synthesis between the meticulous painting and skillful disposition of masses of Antonello da Messina and the poignant graphic art of Mantegna and the contemporary Ferrarese painters. The earliest known works of Vittore Carpaccio, are variously dated between 1480 and 1490: the *Redeemer Giving His Blessing amidst Four Apostles*, which has recently become part of the Moss Collection in Riverdale, the *Portrait of a Man with a Red Cap* in the Museo Correr in Venice, and above all the *Saint Martin Polyptych* in the Museum of Sacred Art in

Zadar. Just where this group of works stands in the stylistic development of Carpaccio is a highly controversial matter, in part owing to the lack of stylistic continuity between the panels, so great that it is thought that the different elements may have been painted at different times.
The most famous of Carpaccio's early works (from the beginning of the last decade of the 15th century) is the panel now in Venice's Museo Correr, entitled *Two Court Ladies* (Plate 1). These are actually two Venetian noblewomen, with refined clothes and hairstyles, seated on a roof terrace. Here the taste for precious detail finds the right balance in an atmosphere of pensive expectation, conveying an impression of silence tinged with melancholy that is reminiscent of certain scenes in the Saint Ursula cycle.
In 1488 the members of the Scuola di Sant'Orsola began to collect funds to be used to celebrate their patron saint with a cycle of paintings. In 1490 Carpaccio signed and dated the *Arrival in Cologne*, the first of the eight canvases that were to be used to decorate the hall of the confraternity, along with the *Apotheosis of the Saint*, an altarpiece that was unusually painted on canvas as well. The execution of these pictures took the artist about five years, and the sequence in which they were painted did not respect that of the story.
In the *King of Brittany Receives the English Ambassadors* (Plate 2), Carpaccio has taken a remarkably free-and-easy approach to the structure of the painting. The scene is organized almost as if it were a triptych whose central "element" is the reception hall of the king. The openings in the background permit the insertion of glimpses of a landscape that is highly characteristic of the Venice lagoon (especially on the left-hand side). On the right, however, Saint Ursula enumerates the conditions for her marriage with the Prince of England.
Following a sequence that alternates large scenes with other, smaller ones, and solemn atmospheres with settings of more delicate absorption, the next scene takes place indoors, and is usually referred to as the *Departure of the Ambassadors* (Plate 3). The indirect light lends warmth to the architectural and decorative elements based on the most up-to-date Venetian practice, the delicate taste of Mauro Codussi and the Lombardo family for extremely refined, patterned and colored marbles.
The *Return of the Ambassadors* (Plate 4) is the canvas that conveys the greatest sense of space, set as it is on the shore of a sort of lagoon. In his handling of the scene, Carpaccio has adapted it to the somewhat theatrical character of the ritual that is taking place and has inserted in a fairly obvious manner the heraldic devices of the noble Compagnia della Calza, a group headed by the Loredan family.
The largest of the scenes represents two episodes: the *Meeting of the Betrothed and the Departure for the Pilgrimage* (Plate 5). A standard, placed almost in the middle, divides the canvas into two parts. A crowd of curious onlookers throngs both sections of the painting and creates a whole of great liveliness. In this, Carpaccio surpasses his master Gentile Bellini, who tends to arrange all his figures in regular sequences and dense ranks.
The *Meeting with the Pope* (Plate 6) takes place in an open space in front of Castel Sant'Angelo: the Mole of Hadrian is painted with a fair amount of accuracy, something that has led people, in the past, to believe that Carpaccio could have visited Rome. In any case, the processions of the prelates and of Saint Ursula's companions, winding in opposite directions, give the scene a depth and spaciousness

comparable with the backgrounds of Piero della Francesca's paintings. It is followed by the most famous canvas in the entire cycle, *Saint Ursula's Dream* (Plate 7): early in the morning, an angel enters the room in which the princess is sleeping, bringing her a vision of her imminent martyrdom. The extremely delicate handling of light in the apparition of the heavenly messenger, the patient and impassioned care with which Carpaccio has depicted the objects in the saint's tranquil room, movingly and tenderly taking them from real life (note the tassel on her pillow, bearing the word *infantia* or "childhood") have provided material for numerous aesthetic and literary interpretations. Quite apart from its profoundly suggestive character, the painting has a special importance: Carpaccio succeeds in creating a pause of silence within the compass of an animated cycle, and obtains an effect of sentimental intimacy thanks to the precise rendering of the light, comparable with that of the *Saint Sebastian* painted in Venice, twenty years earlier, by Antonello da Messina.
The *Arrival in Cologne* (Plates 8, 9) of the galley bearing the betrothed couple and the pope coincides with the siege of the city by the Huns: in this canvas, the smallest and the first in the series to have been painted, there seems already to be a breath of imminent tragedy. It is interesting to note how, along with a number of features that reveal the early date of the painting (and in particular the links with Ercole de Roberti and Ferrarese painting), a number of characteristics are already present that will be found throughout the cycle: the "multiplicity of spatial situations," the lucid wealth of descriptive details, and the ability to maintain a harmonious balance between fantasy and reality.
The series concludes with another double scene, the *Martyrdom and Funeral of Saint Ursula* (Plate 10), who is killed, along with the pope and her companions, in a horrific massacre. Dated 1493, the canvas was painted halfway through the execution of the cycle. Carpaccio makes use of a dense series of cultural references (from Giovanni Bellini to Perugino and Luca Signorelli), but the result is still a personal one. Note the use of a standard to separate the crowded and bloody scene of the martyrdom from the calm serenity of the funeral rites.
The altarpiece, dated 1491, represents Saint Ursula standing on a cluster of palm fronds (a symbol of martyrdom), revered by her companions.

The Legend of Saint George and His Ambivalent Attitude toward Tonality (1495–1510)

During the execution of the canvases for the Scuola di Sant'Orsola, Carpaccio took on and completed a number of other major commissions, and his fame continued to spread.
He gained particular prestige from the *Healing of a Madman* (Plate 12), a picture that was painted as part of a decorative cycle for the Scuola di San Giovanni Evangelista, the work of a variety of artists including Lazzaro Bastiani and Gentile Bellini. All the canvases are now in Venice's Gallerie dell'Accademia. Carpaccio locates the episode of the miracle (which actually took place in Venice in 1494, and is therefore rightly given a contemporary setting) in a loggia of the palace of the patriarch Querini, on the left. The rest of the scene is completely taken up by a view of the Grand Canal, spanned by the Rialto Bridge, then still constructed out of wood.
The *Christ with the Symbols of the Passion Surrounded by Angels* (Plates 13, 14) dates from 1496 and was painted for the

church of San Pietro Martire in Udine, and is now in the Museo Civico of that city.
Around the year 1500, Carpaccio painted the *Sacra Conversazione* (Plate 15), now in the Musée du Petit Palais in Avignon: an imposing arch of rock towers over the main group of figures, while the limpid landscape frames a series of symbolic episodes and a multitude of buildings, many of which appear to be representations of famous actual works of architecture. While the principal figures look a little flat, the natural features, the constructions, and the small figures in the background are extremely vivid: the artist appears to have deliberately taken a stand on behalf of a traditional 15th-century style as opposed to the first signs of the advent of tonalism.
Carpaccio, committed to a "drier," more precise and aristocratic style, seems not to have been interested in the evolution of Venetian painting toward this emphasis on tone. His second great cycle of *teleri*, fortunately still in its original location, is a good demonstration of this, and has all the force of an intensely fascinating group of works. It consists of the episodes painted from 1502 onward in the Scuola di San Giorgio degli Schiavoni (the Slavonians or inhabitants of Dalmatia), depicting scenes from the lives of the Saints Jerome, George, and Tryphon. The multiple dedication, in contrast to the cycle devoted entirely to Saint Ursula, results in a number of scenes being completely disconnected from the others, like the two small panels depicting the *Calling of Saint Matthew* and the *Prayer in the Garden*, from 1502. As in the case of the *Legend of Saint Ursula*, it took Carpaccio about five years to complete the cycle, from 1502 to 1507. The three episodes on the right-hand wall, devoted to Saint Jerome, were among the first to be painted. *Saint Jerome*

Three studies of bishops, drawing. London, British Museum.

Head of a girl, drawing. Oxford, Ashmolean Museum.

Leads the Lion into the Monastery (Plates 17, 18) is a vivacious canvas, in which Carpaccio even permits himself a touch of humor, with the monks fleeing from the apparition of the tamed lion. It is possible that the courtyard of the monastery in which this scene and the following are set is a faithful representation of the complex of the Hospitalers, in the immediate vicinity of the Scuola degli Schiavoni.
The atmosphere of excitement provoked by the arrival of the lion subsides in the canvas depicting the *Funeral of Saint Jerome* (Plate 19), filled on the contrary with an air of restrained and serene melancholy. This impression is reinforced by the presence of numerous animals that, as often happens in Carpaccio's works, are depicted with scientific precision. The same effort to describe objects, faces, instruments, and every other detail with punctilious accuracy can be found again in the celebrated *Saint Augustine's Vision* (Plates 20–22), which can be regarded as belonging to the same series as the preceding two paintings since it shows Saint Jerome appearing as a vision, in the form of a ray of light, to Saint Augustine, who is engrossed in meditation in his study.
Surrounded by the instruments of learning, regularly arranged in an ample, peaceful, and brightly-lit space, Saint Augustine suddenly looks up, lifting his hand for a moment from the parchment, and turns toward the light streaming through the window. Taking its cue from a Venetian text, in which Saint Jerome is said to have appeared and spoken to Saint Augustine in the form of a ray of light, Carpaccio provides another demonstration of his ability to make precise use of sources of light to pick out objects and convey feelings. Yet it is significant that here, as in *Saint Ursula's Dream*, the light is carefully delimited and enters the scene from one side, just at the moment when, with the emergence of tonal painting, an era of diffuse overhead or frontal light was dawning.
Of the last scenes painted in the Scuola degli Schiavoni, the *Miracle of Saint Tryphon* betrays the intervention of assistants, but the three episodes that have Saint George as their protagonist are entirely Carpaccio's work. The canvas depicting *Saint George and the Dragon* (Plate 23) is a typical example of the narrative approach, like that of a tale of chivalry, used by Carpaccio in his *teleri*. The horrifyingly macabre details, the fabulous architecture, the noble and fearless beauty of the saint and his steed, and the anxious gesture of the princess are all ingredients of the fable, still linked to the world of the medieval *chanson de geste*. The *Triumph of Saint George*, on the contrary (Plate 24), showing the saint about to kill the dragon, is in a style of the perspective-Renaissance type, notwithstanding the highly exotic character of the figures. The group of trumpeters and drummers reappears in the next scene, *Saint George Baptizing the People of Silene* (Plates 25, 26), in which many other figures from the *Triumph of Saint George* can also be seen. In addition, the architectural scenery confers a more dignified solemnity on the episode of the baptism.
At the same time as he was painting the canvases for the Scuola degli Schiavoni, Carpaccio was commissioned to execute a cycle devoted to the Madonna by the "rival" Scuola degli Albanesi (School of the Albanians). This is a series of six roughly square canvases depicting scenes from the life of the Virgin Mary, painted between 1502 and 1508: the cycle, which was already in a poor condition in the 18th century, has been dismembered and is now in a variety of museums. It is likely that Carpaccio found the Saint George canvases much more stimulating: in any

case, there is a clear decline in quality in the episodes from Mary's life, which can be attributed in great part to the extensive contribution of collaborators. The best painting is the *Annunciation* (Plate 30), now in the Galleria Franchetti of the Ca' d'Oro, dated April 1504. In all probability this was the second canvas delivered to the Albanesi, after the *Birth of the Virgin* (Plates 28, 29) in the Accademia Carrara in Bergamo, and it can be compared, for the tranquil way in which the composition is handled, to the *Madonna Reading* (Plate 31) in the National Gallery in Washington.

In the cycle depicting the life of Mary, the light seems fainter and the colors softer than in Carpaccio's other works. But this mellowing should not be taken as a sign of his acceptance of the tonal approach. Confirmation of this is provided by a large altarpiece, the *Presentation of Jesus in the Temple*, painted for the church of San Giobbe and now in the Gallerie dell'Accademia. In its present location, as in the original one, Carpaccio's work is hung alongside a *Sacra Conversazione* by Giovanni Bellini, known in fact as the *San Giobbe Altarpiece*. Even though it was painted twenty-three years earlier, Bellini's picture looks if anything more advanced than Carpaccio's. The fact is that, in his desire to depict the magnificent descriptive details (such as the famous angel playing a lute, in the middle) with precision and clarity, Carpaccio has used a cold and steady light, that catches the figures in frozen gestures.

Carpaccio now entered a very delicate phase of his career. His fame was growing: in 1507 he was chosen to paint pictures for the Doge's Palace; in 1508 he was part of a commission of experts appointed to make an evaluation of Giorgione's frescoes in the Fondaco dei Tedeschi, and he sent to Ferrara a *Death of the Virgin*, now in the Pinacoteca Nazionale in Palazzo dei Diamanti; and in 1511 he was in touch with the Gonzaga. And yet his painting was already showing the signs of a deliberate renunciation of the search for new solutions, of a desire to continue his investigation of an artistic direction that had in many ways already been superseded by the evolution of contemporary figurative culture. And his first failures (in 1508 he was defeated in the competition for the execution of the standard of the Scuola della Carità) came alongside moments of austere beauty, in which his apparent "backwardness" produced highly effective results. This was the case with the portrait of a *Knight in a Landscape* (identified as Francesco Maria della Rovere) in the Thyssen-Bornemisza Collection in Madrid (Plate 34), dated 1510, and with the *Presentation in the Temple* (Plate 32): the refined and clear definition of the heraldic details, animals, and symbolic flowers, as well as of the botanical and natural world that surrounds the fascinating figure of the young knight, is a reflection of a descriptive approach that still has a 15th-century flavor, fostered by an extremely limpid light and patient brushwork. As a result, one forgets the undoubted "modernization" of a portrait that is in other ways innovative: the relationship between figure and setting is handled with great intuition; the knight is portrayed full-length, a device that was to become increasingly important in the future but that was almost experimental at the time; and the left arm is reflected in the cuirass, as if the painter wished to make a contribution to the debate under way in Venice about the supremacy of painting over sculpture.

The Last Glimmers before the End (1510–1526)

In 1511 Carpaccio set to work, at a very

slow pace, on a new cycle of *teleri*, this time devoted to Saint Stephen. As in the case of the scenes from the Scuola degli Albanesi, these paintings are now split up among a number of different museums. The painter also relied on the assistance of workshop collaborators. Nevertheless, there are moments of great beauty in the Saint Stephen cycle. Carpaccio's work, it is true, is increasingly inconsistent: some of the paintings reveal a dulling of inspiration, or even the standard use of a repertory of outdated models. But when his involvement is more direct, the artist is still able to achieve accents of astonishingly powerful emotion. The legacy of the Quattrocento, still linked to Mantegna, was reinforced in a way by Dürer's arrival in Venice, rendering even more intense two works with similar subjects that are difficult to date accurately: the *Meditation on the Dead Christ* in the Metropolitan Museum in New York and the *Preparation for the Entombment of Christ* (Plate 33) in the Staatliche Museen of Berlin. In both paintings, a landscape strewn with tragical human remains, as rugged and rocky as the harshest of the fantasies of Mantegna or the Ferrarese painters, contains silent scenes of anguish and death. The lucid clarity of the forms, emphasized by clean and sharp outlines, gives this work a quality of visionary hallucination that has a powerful effect on the onlooker.

Naturally the scenes from the life of Saint Stephen are less harsh: a common characteristic of all the canvases in the cycle is the presence of buildings with a complex and elaborate structure, not lacking in direct references to antiquity. The most successful episode is the *Disputation of Saint Stephen* (Plate 35), dated 1514 and now in the Pinacoteca di Brera in Milan. In that same year of 1514, some far less successful works were coming out of Carpaccio's workshop. Among these were the labored *Santa Fosca Polyptych*, whose panels are now split up among various museums, and the equally involved altarpiece of the *Glory of Saint Vitalis* (Plate 36), in the Venetian church of San Vitale, an interesting but monotonous pastiche of standard motifs and models.

Carpaccio's last brilliant creation, the *Ten Thousand Crucifixions of Mount Ararat* (Plate 37), formerly in Sant'Antonio di Castello and now in the Gallerie dell'Accademia, dates from 1515. Probably taking his inspiration from the works of Dürer and the drawings of Michelangelo, but above all summoning up an inventive energy that had clearly not faded, Carpaccio composes a macabre but extremely vivid scene, mixing exotic figures with an infinity of male nudes.

One of the last works painted by Carpaccio in Venice is filled with symbolic meanings: this is the *Lion of Saint Mark* (Plate 38), dated 1516, formerly in the Palazzo dei Camerlenghi and now in the Doge's Palace. It presents a faithful view of the Basin of Saint Mark, while the winged lion of the Serenissima is set halfway between the sea and the land, signifying Venice's dominion over both. In the lower part appear the coats of arms of five noble families.

In the last ten years of his life, at a time when the star of Titian had already risen in Venice, Carpaccio realized that he was no longer capable of renewing his own style. He completed, in a more than decorous manner, the Saint Stephen cycle and then devoted himself mainly to works for the provinces, often relying on the collaboration of his workshop, and his son Benedetto in particular: a *Saint Paul* for the Chioggia Cathedral (1520), a polyptych for the parish church of Pozzale, near Pieve di Cadore, and a large number of paintings for Istria and Dalmatia: the churches of Piran and Koper provided a home for his last works. With these pathetic mementoes of an age that was now irremediably over, and that had perhaps passed all too quickly, Carpaccio's life drew to an end. His death came between October 1525 and June 1526.

The Legacy

Carpaccio's influence on the evolution of subsequent Venetian painting is far from apparent. Even the genre of the narrative *teleri*, so congenial to Carpaccio, went into decline over the course of the 15th century, until it disappeared altogether. So the pupils in his studio (his sons Paolo and Benedetto, Francesco Bissolo, Giovanni Mansueti, and even Lazzaro Bastiani) were unable to take it any further after the master's death.

It is interesting to note that this "surpassing" of Carpaccio's figurative culture was matched by a degree of perplexity among the critics. An embarrassment with regard to Carpaccio is fairly evident in all the 16th-century writers on art. He was usually placed, but without a great deal of conviction, alongside Giovanni Bellini, or regarded as his pupil. A number of works received unanimous praise (especially the *Legend of Saint Ursula*), but no one attempted a historical reconstruction of his biography.

Admiration for the painter's "diligence" came into conflict, throughout the 17th century, with criticism of the "stiffness" of a style that still belonged to the late-15th-century. Even in the 18th century Carpaccio remained in a sort of critical limbo. Lanzi himself, in spite of the "rehabilitation" proposed only a few years earlier by Zanetti and the obvious revival of Carpaccio's motifs on the part of the veduta painters, was unable to get over this difficulty.

The definitive "discovery" of Carpaccio would be left to the foreign travelers of the 19th century, and especially Ruskin. Modern criticism of Carpaccio commenced with the monograph published in 1906 by Ludwig and Molmenti, which was followed by the researches carried out by Venturi, Berenson, and Fiocco. Largely thanks to the efforts of this last scholar, we have begun to see Carpaccio in the light of a new cultural complexity. Little by little, the old view of a painter of "fables" has given way to a critical interpretation that is more probing and yet no less interesting for that. It is to Longhi that we owe our understanding of the influence of Antonello da Messina and Piero della Francesca on the spatial complexity of the scenes composed by Carpaccio. The beginning of the sixties, with the staging of a major exhibition of his work in Venice in 1963, saw a resurgence of critical interest. Lauts must be given the credit for a new catalogue of the works and for a reappraisal of the drawings. The contributions of Pignatti, Perocco, Zampetti, and Muraro led, around 1970, to a fundamental stabilization of the situation. Successive interventions, including the adventurous literary, symbolic, and philosophical interpretation of Serres and the establishment of a link between the *Legend of Saint Ursula* and the theater on the part of Zorzi, have attempted to deepen our understanding of the historico-critical terms of Carpaccio's culture. More recently, Humfrey has put together a new and updated catalogue of the artist's paintings.

Where to See Carpaccio

Today around seventy works by Carpaccio are known to us, about half of them panels and half canvases. This number may have to be adjusted on the basis of the attribution of a few doubtful paintings, especially from his juvenile period, which has not been fully confirmed.
We have an essentially complete picture of the course taken by the artist in the mature period of his career and his activity in Venice between 1490 and 1520 can be followed almost in its entirety. Even the closing years of his life, which were spent in Dalmatia, can now be reconstructed through the surviving works from this time. This is largely due to the good state of preservation of several important cycles of large canvases (in their original locations or in the Gallerie dell'Accademia di Venezia) and to an impressive series of altarpieces.
Yet there are a number of gaps in the story and paintings that have vanished.
The old sources record the presence of works of some importance in Venice that can no longer be traced or that have been destroyed at various times.
The greatest source of regret is the loss of two works linked to the legend of Barbarossa and Pope Alexander III, painted for the Hall of the Great Council in the Doge's Palace and destroyed by fire in 1577. In addition, it is worth mentioning two altarpieces (a triptych for SS. Giovanni e Paolo and a *Madonna with Donors* in the Scuola dei Tessitori) that were destroyed between the 18th and 19th centuries, and a series of works painted for the patriarchate of San Pietro di Castello. The majority of Carpaccio's pictures were painted for public institutions: churches, *Scuole* (guildhalls), and other civil bodies. Unfortunately, however, only a few of the paintings have remained in their original locations: the breakup of groups of canvases has resulted in the dispersion of series that were intended to be seen as a whole but are now split up among different museums in different countries.

Works in Italy

About two-thirds of Carpaccio's works are still in Italy, the vast majority of them in Venice. Although almost all of them have been moved from their original locations, Carpaccio's paintings are closely linked to their Venetian birthplace, in a relationship that works in both directions. Carpaccio's canvases mirror a happy age in the Republic's history; and, at the same time, the light, architecture, customs, and figures of daily life on the city's alleys and bridges were a continual source of inspiration for the painter.

Venice

There can be no doubt that the best starting point for a tour of the city in search of paintings by Carpaccio is the Scuola di San Giorgio degli Schiavoni. The series of large canvases representing *Scenes from the Life of Saint George, Saint Jerome, Saint Matthew, Saint Augustine, and Saint Tryphon* (the patron saints of the Confraternity of Dalmatians) has been preserved in its entirety, although it is now displayed in a different room from the one in which it was originally located. The fact that these canvases are still

housed in the 16th-century setting of the guildhall makes them one of the most fascinating groups of Venetian paintings from the Renaissance.
The cycle depicting *Scenes from the Life of Saint Ursula* (1490-1495) is no less interesting. The building of the Scuola di Sant'Orsola is still standing but in very poor condition: the pictures have been moved to a special room in the Gallerie dell'Accademia, where they have been arranged in their original sequence. Thus the alternation of episodes of calm contemplation with moments of lively action has been fully preserved.
The Gallerie dell'Accademia contains another famous cycle of canvases from a guildhall: the *Miracles of the Cross* from the Scuola di San Giovanni Evangelista. To this joint undertaking by the Venetian school of painters, Carpaccio contributed the *Healing of a Madman*, a scene which is set on the bank of the Grand Canal with a view of the Rialto Bridge.
Venice's main museum contains a number of other works by Carpaccio that are of considerable importance: the *Presentation in the Temple*, dated 1510 and originally in San Giobbe, is fundamental to an understanding of the painter's evolution in the field of the altarpiece; the panel depicting the *Ten Thousand Crucifixions Mount Ararat* displays a surprising virtuosity; the *Apparition of the Martyrs to Saint Peter of Castello* provides a precious record of the interior of a Venetian church in the Renaissance.
Two churches still contain works by Carpaccio: San Vidal has the altarpiece depicting *Saint Vitalis between Other Saints* (1514), while the Sala del Conclave in San Giorgio Maggiore houses *Saint George and the Dragon*, a later version of the similar scene in the Scuola degli Schiavoni.
The proud canvas depicting the *Lion of Saint Mark*, formerly in the Palazzo dei Camerlenghi, is now on display in the Doge's Palace.
The Galleria Franchetti in the Ca' d'Oro possesses two elegant canvases from the cycle of scenes from the life of Mary originally in the Scuola degli Albanesi: the *Annunciation* and the *Death of the Virgin*. A third scene from the series, the *Visitation*, can be seen in the Museo Correr, along with a number of important early paintings such as the disputed *Portrait of a Man with a Red Cap* and the so-called *Courtesan*. With the late altarpiece representing *Saint Paul* in the church of San Domenico at Chioggia, the list of works by Carpaccio in the Venetian area is complete.

Lombardy
A fair number of works by Carpaccio can be found in the province of *Bergamo* (formerly a possession of the Venetian Republic) and in the Pinacoteca di Brera in *Milan*.
The parish church of *Grumello de' Zanchi (Bergamo)* houses an unusual *Polyptych*, in all likelihood made up of panels taken from different groups of pictures. The Galleria dell'Accademia Carrara, in Bergamo, has another scene from the cycle painted for the Scuola degli Albanesi, the *Birth of the Virgin*. It also has the *Portrait of Doge Loredan* and an altarpiece with *Six Saints*, which was originally split into three parts to form a triptych.
There are two more canvases from the Albanesi series in Brera, the *Presentation of Mary in the Temple* and the *Wedding of the Virgin*. The glowing *Preaching of Saint Stephen* (1514), from the Scuola dei Lanieri, is a more accomplished work.

Other Places in Italy
There are few works by Carpaccio located outside the cities already mentioned, and none of them are of very great importance.
In the former Venetian territories, it is worth mentioning the altarpiece depicting *Christ Giving His Blood* in the Museo Civico of Udine. Then there are the *Two Saints* in the Museo di Castelvecchio at Verona and the feeble and late *Polyptych* in the parish church of Pozzale di Cadore.
The Pinacoteca Nazionale in *Ferrara* has a *Death of the Virgin* that was originally in the local church of Santa Maria in Vado. Still in Emilia, there is the *Dead Christ Supported by Angels* in the Fondazione Magnani Rocca at *Mamiano (Parma)*.
Finally, the Galleria degli Uffizi in *Florence* contains a group of *Halberdiers*, a fragment of a larger composition.

Works Abroad
When speaking of the distribution of Carpaccio's pictures outside Italy, a distinction has to be made between two different situations. In Istria and Dalmatia it is still possible to find works or parts of groups that were painted for their current locations.
Other works have found their way abroad as a result of purchases made by collectors, even in recent times. Typical of this phenomenon is the substantial number of paintings by Carpaccio that are now in collections in the United States.

Istria and Dalmatia
The Museum of Sacred Art in *Zadar* houses the large *Saint Martin Polyptych*, perhaps the most complex of Carpaccio's works to be found in the former Yugoslavia.
The Cathedral of Our Lady of the Assumption in *Koper* still has parts of the organ doors (*Presentation of Christ in the Temple*, *Slaughter of the Innocents*) and an altarpiece with a *Sacra Conversazione* (1516), a sort of belated recapitulation of the compositional motifs of the Madonna and saints of the 15th-century tradition. In the Municipal museum of the same city there are other portions of the organ doors and the "civic" canvas depicting the *Entrance of the Podestà Sebastiano Contarini into Koper*.
A late altarpiece can be seen in the church of Saint Francis at *Piran*.
The Strossmayer Gallery in *Zagreb* contains a *Saint Sebastian*, the central element of a triptych painted in 1514 whose lateral sections (*Saint Roche* and *Saint Peter the Martyr*) are in the Accademia Carrara in Bergamo and the Museo Correr in Venice.
There are two panels representing *Saint Sebastian* and *Saint Rock*, of uncertain origin, in the National Museum in *Belgrade*.

Germany
There are fine paintings by Carpaccio in a number of German museums. The most fascinating of these works is the *Preparation for the Entombment of Christ* in the Staatliche Museen in *Berlin*, which also possesses the *Consecration of Saint Stephen*, originally part of the cycle in the Scuola dei Lanieri. Another painting from the same series, the *Martyrdom of Saint Stephen*, is in the Staatsgalerie in *Stuttgart*, along with the altarpiece depicting *Saint Thomas Enthroned*, originally located in *Murano*.
In *Frankfurt* there is a delicate *Madonna and Child and the Young Saint John*, while the *Madonna between Saint Catherine and Saint Jerome*, in the manner of Bellini, is in the Kunsthalle in *Karlsruhe*.

United States
The Metropolitan Museum of Art in *New York* possesses one of Carpaccio's most intense paintings, the *Meditation on the Dead Christ*. An unusual "genre" picture can be seen at the Getty Museum in *Malibu*, the *Hunt on the Lagoon*, which has several letters painted on the back in *tromp-l'œil*.
There are three fine works in the National Gallery in *Washington*: the extremely delicate *Madonna* (or *Saint*) *Reading*, a serene *Madonna and Child*, and the *Flight into Egypt*.
Further confirmation of Carpaccio's great popularity with American collectors is provided by the two portraits of women in *Denver* and *Kansas City*, the *Christ Giving His Blessing* in *New Orleans*, the *Holy Family* in *Tucson*, the *Four Saints in Tulsa*, the *Myth of Alcyone* in *Philadelphia*, the *Two Virtues* in *Atlanta*, and above all the *Salvator mundi* in *Riverdale*, the earliest known work by the painter.

Other Locations
Only a few more notes are required to complete our survey of the distribution of Carpaccio's works.
There are three important paintings in France: the *Preaching of Saint Stephen*, from the Lanieri cycle, is in the Musée du Louvre in Paris; another work in the capital is the canvas depicting the mythological subject of *Theseus and the Queen of the Amazons*, in the Musée Jacquemart André; finally, the Musée du Petit Palais in *Avignon* has a complex *Holy Family*, rich in subtle symbology.
The Gulbenkian Foundation in *Lisbon* possesses an excellent *Adoration of the Child with Two Donors*.
Finally, the Thyssen-Bornemisza Collection, which has recently transferred from Lugano to *Madrid*, boasts the most important of Carpaccio's portraits, the *Knight in a Landscape*. The subject has been identified as Francesco Maria della Rovere.

1

2

Preceding page
1. Two Court Ladies,
ca. 1490, panel, 94 × 64 cm. Venice, Museo Correr.
The traditional title is deceptive: the picture is really of two noblewomen, attired and adorned according to the Venetian fashion of the last decade of the 15th century. It is possible that the left-hand part of the painting has been cut off, but it retains all its charm owing to the atmosphere of melancholy that it emanates. As was to become typical of Carpaccio, the scene is enlivened by numerous animals.

Cycle of the Scuola di Sant'Orsola (Legend of Saint Ursula), *1490–1494, nine canvases, Venice, Gallerie dell'Accademia.*
This is the most famous group of paintings by Carpaccio, preserved in its entirety although no longer in its original location (alongside the basilica of SS. Giovanni e Paolo). The probable influences on his training (Gentile Bellini's feeling for narrative, Antonello da Messina's sense of space, Alvise Vivarini's precise use of light, the clear-cut graphics of the Ferrarese) appear to have been superseded by a style that is increasingly confident and personal. With subtle ambiguity, Carpaccio maintains a balance between reality and fantasy,

creating the impression of a fairy-tale Venice, which provides the setting for the romantic and sad story of the beautiful Princess Ursula. Even the cadences of the composition are in tune with the rhythm of this fascinating courtly tale. We give the traditional titles, following the sequence of the legend, which does not correspond to the chronological order of their execution. They are in a good state of preservation.

2. The King of Brittany Receives the English Ambassadors, *ca. 1495, canvas, 275 × 589 cm.*
Applying the geometric rigor of Renaissance perspective to the vast resources of his own inventiveness as a scene painter, Carpaccio constructs a scene rich in spatial effects, with an endless variety of solutions.
The ambassadors deliver a letter asking for the hand of Princess Ursula in marriage for the hereditary English prince.
In the right-hand part of the painting, Ursula, in her own room, details her conditions for the marriage to her father, while the elderly nurse, at the foot of the steps, already seems to have a presentiment of her future martyrdom.
The painting is filled with a multitude of invaluable observations of a documentary character.

3

3. Departure of the Ambassadors, *ca. 1495, canvas, 280 × 253 cm. The scene appears to be set inside a royal chancellory: the formal gestures of the ambassadors are matched by the sumptuous decoration of the setting, with patterned slabs of multicolored marble that record the Venetian style of architecture and decoration at the end of the 15th century. The use of light is very skillful, defining the objects in space with precise rigor, as can be seen in the gleaming brass chandelier.*

4

4. Return of the Ambassadors, *ca. 1495, canvas, 297 × 527 cm. The galley of the ambassadors is moored, on the left, alongside a wharf that recalls the Arsenal in Venice, just as the whole architectural and natural setting is reminiscent of the lagoon. The movements of the messengers, determined by ritual, are observed by a genuine crowd of curious bystanders, lining the banks.*

While the rhythms of the scene and the opulent costumes seem to be derived from the theater, the architectural and ornamental details are drawn from an austere and up-to-date repertory of Renaissance models, close to Humanistic tastes; but Carpaccio is also capable of adding a touch of humor, with the monkey dressed as a jester and teasing a strutting guinea fowl, on the steps of the royal pavilion.

5. The Meeting of the Betrothed and the Departure for the Pilgrimage, *1495, canvas, 280 × 611 cm. This is the largest of the canvases: a standard, set almost in the middle, divides it neatly into two parts. A skillful blend of real and imaginary elements, which probably includes numerous portraits of people who actually existed, lends verisimilitude to a setting that has the charm of a fairy tale. In spite of the combination of two quite distinct episodes and the dilatation of space, Carpaccio keeps a firm grip on the thread of the story.*

5

6

6. The Meeting with the Pope, *ca. 1493, canvas, 281 × 387 cm. The scene is rendered particularly solemn by the convergence of the two processions (the companions of Saint Ursula and the prelates in the pope's retinue) as they make their way toward the open ground where Pope Ciriaco greets and blesses the betrothed couple, who have fallen to their knees. The remarkable accuracy with which Castel Sant'Angelo is painted has led pople to suggest that Carpaccio visited Rome: but the monument was very well-known, in part through printed reproductions. The range of colors lays particular emphasis on white and red, as if in a noble heraldic device.*

7

7. Saint Ursula's Dream, *1495, canvas, 274 × 267 cm. A fascinating demonstration of versatility on the part of Carpaccio, who passes from scenes with a tone of dignified austerity to this episode of touching intimacy. An angel with the palm of martyrdom, enters early in the morning into the room in which Ursula is sleeping, bringing her a warning of her imminent death in a dream.*
The objects and furnishings that surround the peacefully sleeping saint are depicted with loving and touching care, and represent an extremely faithful reproduction of a wealthy Venetian house at the end of the 15th century.

8

8, 9. Arrival in Cologne, *1490, canvas, 280 × 255 cm. This was the first of the canvases to be painted, and in fact still displays a slight awkwardness in the execution of some figures and a certain amount of confusion in the architecture. Saint Ursula and the pope peer out of the ship on the left and receive the news that the city of Cologne is under siege by the Huns. With this canvas Carpaccio inaugurated his own, highly personal narrative style, made up of a blend of reality and fantasy and of penetrating symbolic allusions.*

10

10. Martyrdom and Funeral of Saint Ursula, *1493, canvas, 271 × 561 cm.*
The savage scene of the martyrdom of the saint, her companions, and the pope is balanced, in the right-hand part, by the calm ceremony of the funeral.
As in other canvases of the cycle, Carpaccio is able to create a harmony between two completely different scenes within the same picture, without any abrupt breaks.
Among the figures attending the funeral, there are portraits of the members of the Scuola di Sant'Orsola, the clients for the cycle.

11

12

11. Apotheosis of Saint Ursula, *1491, canvas, 481 × 336 cm.*
Intended as an altarpiece for the seat of the School, it is undoubtedly the least convincing part of the whole cycle. The structure of the composition appears conventional, and the tenderness of the martyrs somewhat contrived. However, there is considerable technical interest in the use of canvas as a support for an altarpiece, something that was highly unusual for the end of the Quattrocento.

12. The Healing of a Madman, *1494, canvas, 365 × 389 cm. Venice, Gallerie dell'Accademia.*
The episode forms part of a complex cycle of canvases depicting Stories of the True Cross, painted, as well as by Carpaccio, by Gentile Bellini, Lazzaro Bastiani, and other specialists in narrative painting. It was a truly unique opportunity for Carpaccio, in that the subject represents a miracle that took place in Venice in 1494. The accurate portrayal of the Grand Canal, with the Rialto Bridge still built out of wood, is therefore perfectly justified by the subject. The miracle actually occurs on the roof terrace on the left, but the greater part of the canvas is taken up by an effective "live" depiction of contemporary Venice, almost an anticipation of the work of the Venetian "veduta" painters of the Settecento.

14

13, 14. Christ with the Symbols of the Passion Surrounded by Angels, *1496, canvas, 162 × 160 cm. Udine, Museo Civico.*
The theme of the Sacrifice of the Mass was a very popular one in the religious life and figurative culture of Veneto at the end of the 15th century. It is very unusual, however, to see it represented on a large scale, as in this case.
It is a plausible hypothesis that the castle on the right is that of Udine, included as a homage to the city for which the picture was painted.

15

15. Sacra Conversazione, *ca. 1500, panel, 98 × 127 cm. Avignon, Musée du Petit Palais.*
The date and the exact subject of this unusual composition, rich in symbolism, are fairly controversial. The idea for the iconography may have come from a theme typical of northern European painting, the Holy Relatives, with children playing while their mothers are engaged in housework. The arch of rock that spans the group, the tiny figures scattered through the landscape, and the buildings of the city in the background are handled with a limpid sense of detail.

16

16. The Dead Christ Supported by Angels, *ca. 1502, panel, 62 × 62 cm. Mamiano (Parma), Fondazione Magnani Rocca. This is one of the few cases in which Carpaccio succeeds in finding accents of authentic poetry in a non-narrative subject. Evidently, as was to be confirmed in other, later works, the theme of the lament over the dead Christ stimulated him to seek his own solutions, and to reproduce them in new settings: the head and bust of Christ were to be used again, in the* Meditation on the Dead Christ *in New York.*

17

Cycle of the Scuola di San Giorgio degli Schiavoni, *1502–1507, series of canvases.*
This is the only group of canvases by Carpaccio that have remained in the building they were originally painted for.
A center for Dalmatians living in Venice, the School was devoted to three saints: Jerome, George, and Tryphon. As a result, Carpaccio's paintings do not in this case recount the story of a single personage, but depict episodes from the life of the different patron saints. It is very likely that the Knights of Rhodes, whose seat was close to the School, gave considerable economic assistance to Carpaccio's clients.
In this connection, attention has been drawn to the "chivalrous" and noble character of the scenes from the life of Saint George, an ideal model for the aristocratic knights. The Slavonians, who were not rich, might not have been able to afford an artist like Carpaccio.

17, 18. Saint Jerome Leads the Lion into the Monastery, *1502, canvas, 141 × 211 cm.*
With considerable humor, Carpaccio depicts the headlong flight of the monks on the appearance of the lion tamed by Saint Jerome, who looks perplexed by such a terror-stricken reaction.
The long habits of the fleeing monks seem to dilate the space of the monastery courtyard in which the scene takes place.

19

19. Funeral of Saint Jerome, *1502, canvas, 141 × 211 cm. The silence and calm of the monastery provide the setting for this serene portrayal of the funeral of Saint Jerome, who is laid out on the ground. The animals grazing in the courtyard almost seem to be participating, with their tranquillity, in the intimacy and dignity of the sacred rite.*

20

20–22. Saint Augustine's Vision, *1502–1504, canvas, 141 × 211 cm.*
The scene is part of the cycle devoted to Saint Jerome: it records the appearance of the saint, in the form of a ray of light, in Saint Augustine's study.
Inspired by the idea of this luminous vision, Carpaccio has structured the whole scene around the impalpable effulgence that filters through the windows located on the right and softly fills the room. Not only Saint Augustine, but even the little furry dog and all the objects in the study seem entranced by the miraculous light, transfixed in a moment of intense mysticism. Yet, and this is where the power of the painting lies, it is really only the natural light of the everyday world, gentle and penetrating, that illuminates and outlines all the instruments of science and learning by which Saint Augustine is surrounded, producing a vivid and realistic rendering of the study of a Humanist.

21

23. Saint George and the Dragon, *1504–1507, canvas, 141 × 360 cm.*
Here is the culminating moment of Saint George's life: in order to set the princess free, the noble knight confronts and strikes the terrible dragon. The characteristics of the scene lend themselves to a chivalrous interpretation of the episode, and Carpaccio sticks to the tradition. The contrast between the macabre human remains around the dragon and the fabulous landscape in the background creates a remarkable effect.

24. Triumph of Saint George, *1504–1507, canvas, 141 × 360 cm.*
Along with the preceding canvas, this is the largest in the cycle, and Carpaccio makes use of its elongated shape to isolate the figure of Saint George, who is getting ready to kill the wounded dragon, in the middle. The exotic opulence of the costumes are given a theatrical setting by the fairly simple compositional structure of the architectural background, which may be an echo of central Italian paintings.

23

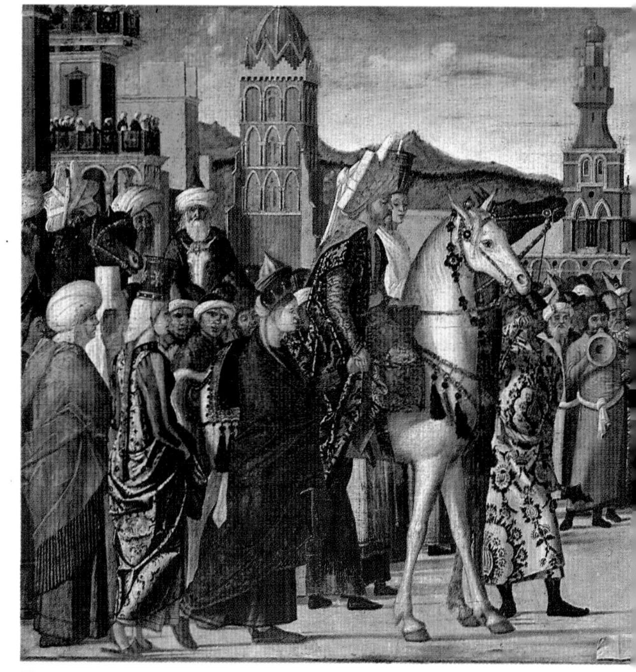

24

25

26

27

25, 26. Saint George Baptizing the People of Silene, *1507, canvas, 141 × 285 cm.*
The curious stance of the young saint, who appears to be preoccupied with not getting himself wet with the baptismal water, somewhat relieves the tension of the painting. Other pleasing digressions include the animals and the white turban deposited on the temple steps, while a celebrated fanfare of trumpets is blaring out on the left.

27. Saint Tryphon and the Basilisk, *ca. 1507, canvas, 163 × 348 cm.*
Patron saint of the Slavonians, Saint Tryphon is very rarely represented in art. For this canvas, one of the last to be painted in the School, Carpaccio has relied on the help of assistants, but he does not hesitate to intervene with his customary wealth of inventiveness in the buildings and the details of the figures. The diffuse luminosity is handled with great care.

28

28, 29. Birth of the Virgin, *1502, canvas, 126 × 129 cm. Bergamo, Accademia Carrara. This was probably the first canvas painted by Carpaccio for the Scuola degli Albanesi. Rivals of the Dalmatians, the Albanians commissioned a cycle of canvases—now located in different Italian museums—from Carpaccio at the same time as he was working on the Scuola di San Giorgio. Because of this, he entrusted much of the work to pupils and studio collaborators.*
The birth of the Virgin takes place inside the house of a well-to-do family of Venetian Jews and the abundance of realistic details fully justifies Berenson's view of Carpaccio as a precursor of "genre" painting.

29

30

30. Annunciation, *1504, canvas, 127 × 139 cm. Venice, Galleria Franchetti in the Ca d'Oro. This canvas is also part of the cycle for the Scuola degli Albanesi. The elaborate entrance to the Virgin's room records the taste for decorated architecture typical of Venetian culture in the early Renaissance.*

31. The Madonna Reading, *ca. 1505, panel transferred onto canvas, 78 × 51 cm. Washington, National Gallery of Art. This is a fragment of a larger composition, which must also have comprised the* Child Seated on a Cushion *at the very least. The air of peaceful concentration is in tune with the psychology of the scenes in the cycle of the Scuola degli Albanesi.*

31

32

33

32. Presentation in the Temple, *1510, panel, 421 × 236 cm. Venice, Gallerie dell'Accademia. This is the best-known and most important of the altarpieces painted by Carpaccio. Originally in the church of San Giobbe, it is based on the 15th-century scheme of the* Sacra Conversazione: *all the figures are set within the niche of an apse decorated with mosaics. Even the precise geometrical definition of the objects (such as the steps on which the famous angel playing a lute is seated, in the middle) is a deliberate reference to the figurative culture of the Quattrocento.*

33. The Preparation for the Entombment of Christ (Meditation on the Dead Christ), *ca. 1510, canvas, 145 × 185 cm. Berlin, Staatliche Museen. The presence of Job (behind Christ, under the tree) connects this painting with the similar scene in New York. Here the atmosphere is perhaps even more forbidding, with the body of Christ laid out on a funeral table in a graveyard strewn with macabre human remains. The figures, working on the preparation of the Holy Sepulchre, and the arid appearance of the landscape convey a chilling sense of mortality.*

34

35

34. Knight in a Landscape, *1510, canvas, 218 × 151 cm. Madrid, Thyssen-Bornemiza Collection.*
Carpaccio was a portrait painter of considerable standing, but this painting stands far above other examples of the genre and has become almost the symbol of a chivalrous age that was drawing to a close. The heraldic devices and other details have suggested the highly plausible theory that the figure portrayed is the twenty-year-old Francesco Maria della Rovere, the future Duke of Urbino.
It is undeniable that the painting is still characterized by a 15th-century approach to the image: thus the flowers, the animals, and the details of the armor and architecture are depicted with loving enthusiasm. Nevertheless, Carpaccio displays here many signs of a profound renewal of style, starting with the almost unprecedented decision to portray the figure at full-length.

35. Disputation of Saint Stephen, *1514, canvas, 147 × 172 cm. Milan, Pinacoteca di Brera.*
The picture is part of a cycle painted for the Scuola di Santo Stefano, now split up among various museums. The canvases were executed by Carpaccio over the course of the second decade of the Cinquecento, and the intervention of assistants can only be seen in marginal parts: thus the scenes from the life of Saint Stephen present the best evidence of the evolution of Carpaccio's painting toward the end of his life.
The scene in Brera, owing to the penetrating clarity of the light and the highly imaginative architecture, is the best in the cycle.
Alongside the oriental scholars, members of the School are present at Saint Stephen's sermon.

36

36. Glory of Saint Vitalis, *1514, canvas, 445 × 214 cm. Venice, San Vitale. Although at first glance solemn and grandiose, the altarpiece sums up the difficulties faced by Carpaccio in painting pictures for altars. In addition, as is typical of the artist's final years, some of the figures are taken from a rather worn-out repertory of models.*

37. The Ten Thousand Crucifixions of Mount Ararat, *1515, canvas, 307 × 205 cm. Venice, Gallerie dell'Accademia. An impressive composition, for which Carpaccio made use of a wide variety of models, ranging from Michelangelo to Dürer. It is one of the paintings that has stirred the sharpest critical debate: ever since the 15th century, scholars have been divided between those who assign to this canvas the value of a mere academic exercise of virtuosity, and those who see it as a work of real daring, with some highly successful parts. It is certainly one of the last paintings that is entirely the master's own work.*

37

38

38. The Lion of Saint Mark, *1516, canvas, 130 × 368 cm. Venice, Doge's Palace. Carpaccio painted a fair number of works for the Senate of the Venetian Republic, but this is the only well-preserved one. Obviously the lion of Saint Mark has to make use of an iconography consolidated over centuries, but Carpaccio brings it to life by inserting a view of the monuments that face onto the basin of Saint Mark. And it is not without significance that the last important work by one of the artists who has made the greatest contribution to keeping alive the "myth" of Venice should be the historic symbol of the millenary dominion of the Serenissima.*

Anthology of Comments

But Vittore Scarpaccia was really the first of them [the pupils of Giovanni Bellini] to produce works of account: and his earliest works were in the Scuola di Sant'Orsola, where he painted on canvas the majority of the stories that tell of the life and death of that Saint: the labor of whose paintings he was able to carry out so well and with such diligence and art, that he acquired the reputation of a highly accomplished and skilled master [...]. And many pictures that are by his hand in Venice and portraits that are true to life, and others, are highly esteemed, for things done in those times.
(G. Vasari, *Le vite de' più eccellenti pittori, scultori et architettori*, 1568).

At the beginning of his career he had a manner that was rather dry than not, but afterward he softened his style over the course of time, whence he acquired the reputation of an excellent master, since not just in the treatment of the stories, but in that touch of grace that he gives to the appearance of the faces, and for such diligence, that diverges from the total harshness used by the ancients, he makes himself agreeable and pleasing: so that he is fully worthy, for us to collect the works that he left in Venice and elsewhere.
(C. Ridolfi, *Le Meraviglie della pittura*, 1658)

And that Vetor Carpacio so excellent,
as if even the brother of Zambelin,
[Giovanni Bellini]
who has painted with style so outlandish, that little or no deference is shown to him?
If Zambelin has made fine figures
with vague and painstaking coloring,
Carpacio is so exquisite,
that face to face can stand his paintings.
(M. Boschini, *Carta del Navegar Pitoresco*, 1660)

I do not expect people to paint like Carpaccio; but in as much as Carpaccio tried to capture vividly the simple truth on his canvases; and that pictorial license should give force and light, and not obstruct and lose this essential and primary part. Very natural expressions full of innate beauty can be found in the faces of any rank, and either sex, painted in these pictures. Carpaccio really had the truth in his heart.
(A.M. Zanetti, *Della pittura veneziana*, 1771)

Take a pair of field glasses, and look long and hard at the two princely figures riding horses [in the scene of the *Triumph of Saint George*], on the left—the Saracen king, with his high white turban, and his daughter, behind him, with the red headdress, as tall as the tower of a castle. Look at them well, and for a long time. For in truth, and I say this with sure and hard-earned knowledge of the subject, in this whole globe of ours, seeking out all that is most splendid that has been produced by the best of its life you will find nothing that truly equals this little work, for supreme, serene, sure delicacy of the art of painting. In its simplicity it towers above every other precious thing, amongst those with which I

am familiar, since it combines the perfect joy of old age and, at the same time, the strength and splendor of manhood. In varying degrees, this is, in truth, a quality common to the whole of Carpaccio's work and to his mind; but here you see it in a real jewel, radiant and priceless.
(J. Ruskin, *Guide to the Principal Pictures of Venice*, 1877).

However much he loved ceremonial subjects, he was no less happy to paint domestic episodes [...]; even the scene of the "Presentation of the Virgin in the Temple," which offered magnificent opportunities for choreography, Carpaccio, for once, has reduced it to the story of an ordinary girl who is going to receive her first Communion. In other words, the quality typical of Carpaccio is that of the genre painter; in this sense, and in order of time, he was the first of the Italians. His genre differs from the Dutch and the French, in degree more than in kind. The Dutch genre is far more democratic, and as painting is of a much more refined quality; but it interprets the subject, just as Carpaccio does, in view of the pictorial possibilities and the effects of chiaroscuro and color.
(B. Berenson, *The Italian Painters of the Renaissance*, 1896)

Ah, in what pure and poetic sleep rests the Maid Ursula in her immaculate bed! The most benign of silences fills the solitary room in which it seems as if the pious lips of the sleeper mouth the customary prayer.
Through the half-open doors and windows penetrates the timid light of dawn, and illuminates the word written on the corner of the pillow. "Childhood," is the simple word, that sheds a freshness similar to that of the morning around the head of the maid. INFANTIA. Already betrothed to the pagan prince and promised to martyrdom, the virgin sleeps. Is not she, chaste, ingenuous, and ardent, the very picture of Art as it was seen by our forerunners with the sincerity of their childlike eyes?
(G. D'Annunzio, *Il fuoco*, 1898)

Bright as the setting sun are the canvases of Carpaccio, in which everything—from the man to the hanging stocking, to the stunted blade of grass, to the gigantic cuckoo-pint, to the waving pennant, to the minaret, and to the brightly-colored architecture of his friends Coducci and Lombardi—everything casts its shadow further as a surer confirmation. Here in the *Saint George* the terrible fork of shadow beneath the dragon is already just like the shadow under the gate. But who does not recall the pointer of shade that, in a funnel of light, precedes the angel as she slips, with her back to the rising sun, into Ursula's room? Or the bent shadows of the railings in the *Reception of the Ambassadors*? Or the sharply pointed triangle of shadow of the little dog in St. Augustine's study? Or the spikes of shadow attached to every object on the Saint's shelves? This it seems to me is the last element of persuasion that comes from Carpaccio and that gives to everyone of his tales its supreme, epic indifference, its open clarity.
Let us look then with a light heart at each different event and every detail will turn out to be necessary: the tilting of the bishops' mitres at the reception of St. Ursula in the Prati di Castello under the Mole of Hadrian; the foreshortened flank of the long walls of Cologne; the clear and complicated carnage at the edge of the municipal woods; the bier of the martyr that is lifted and borne toward the bright and festive light; the blanching faces of the people as they set off on their journey against the dark green water; the speckled liveries of the gondoliers on the dark Grand Canal, under a windswept sky; the gondola for Murano that looks as if it is suspended on the clear water. And Carpaccio, a lucid spectator who does not bat an eyelid, does not become involved, but just depicts: a preordained world though, its parts already arranged: from the ever-changing rustle of the enormous flower-patterned ceremonial robe in the foreground to the more distant spot of the citizen who was not even invited to the ceremony and so is slipping away.
(R. Longhi, *Viatico per cinque secoli di pittura veneziana*, 1946)

It will suffice to make a more careful comparison [between the narrative canvases of Gentile Bellini and those of Carpaccio] to recognize Carpaccio's extraordinary "architectural" quality, which leads him to string figure on figure, along the picturesque fronts of the palaces on the Grand Canal, with an unflagging sense of distance and of volumes in space, leav-

ing us speechless and spellbound. See how the accordion of the windows and balconies is reduced to blades of light, on the foreshortened facades to the left [in the *Miracle of the Madman* in the Gallerie dell'Accademia]; or look for the luministic effects, as carefully gauged as in a technical drawing, even an engineer's blueprint, of the bridge's piers; or note the dazzling facets of the reflections on the steps of the banks, where the gondolas come alongside, drawn by invisible threads over the slate-like surface of the water... Is it not, all this, something more than the simple "portrait of the city" to which Gentile has accustomed us? Does it not attain, instead, a mysterious, theoretical "geometry?" Here is the "abstract" point that lies at the foundation of Carpaccio's stylistic construction, and that renders his paintings so agreeable, at a time in which architecture was undoubtedly the most lively of artistic languages, while its rational demands rigidly led the inspiration of figurative artists away from the path of reality, seen in its unmotivated physical aspects. Carpaccio an "abstract" artist? In this sense, undoubtedly.
(T. Pignatti, *Vittore Carpaccio*, 1963)

Everyone has found themselves, at least once, while strolling down a road where they have been before, or wandering around a familiar part of town, observing it, discovering its details as if for the very first time, entrances, stores, windows, signs, cornices, and gutters, enjoying it piece by piece, caught up in the pure pleasure of looking. Well, I think that this is the best way to understand the painting of Carpaccio. His pictures ask no more than what reality asks of him: to allow themselves to be seen, to allow themselves be discovered, without anything being left out.
(M. Cancogni, "Più fantastico di una favola," in *L'opera completa del Carpaccio*, 1967)

Carpaccio's settings, while extremely Venetian in their spirit, are completely fantastic and any reference to real situations is scrupulously avoided. Obviously this is not an attempt to get away from the history of Venice, but to take part in it in a higher and more creative form, not as a reflection, but as a protagonist of its utopian projection into the future, interpreting its dream, its active ferment. In short, it is a visionary alternative, in which the existing is expanded, integrated, and surpassed.
(G.L. Mellini, *Milano. Pinacoteca di Brera*, 1970)

One sees very few *Annunciations* in which the Virgin is not placed next to an open window or beneath a spacious portico. Cipher of the gift, of abandonment, of welcome, and of faith.
Written code of a spoken yes. The angel, the bird, the ray of light slip, confidently, through this opening. Here we have another annunciation, where the Virgin is not the Virgin, where the angel bears a message of death and not fecundity, where the yes is hidden behind the gates of sleep. Ursula sleeps in the glow before dawn. A bed without curtains, shutters pulled back, doors and windows open. Her eyes are closed, turned toward the East. The Golden Legend tells that she is dreaming. The picture in its turn implies a legend. Under her pillow, as if hanging from its fringe, a small white sphere half in the shade bears the word *infantia*. But not written all in one piece, rather divided into three syllables: IN-FAN-NTIA. Through repetition of the N. A stroke of genius. Ursula is young, to be sure, but betrothed; she is not, or is no longer, a child. So this is the key to the vision. The dream is about her childhood. The dream concerns the word, this word split up in such a way as to say the word spoken and the impossibility of saying it. IN, the negative in the shade, and FAN, that which is pronounced or announced, in the light. She dreams and returns to her childhood, to language and non-language. An exact way of understanding any dream. It is an annunciation and it is not. It is an enunciation and it is not.
(M. Serres, *Esthétiques sur Carpaccio*, 1975)

The scene [of *Christ with the Symbols of the Passion*, Plate 14] is constructed with architectural rigor, on the severe framework provided by Brunelleschi, certainly borrowed from Piero della Francesca's laws of perspective-spatial synthesis (not without references, in the geometric relationships and plastic values, to the lexicon of Antonello). Yet there is also a perceptible desire for critical regeneration, as is apparent from the inspired use of diverging lines (the poles and the cross) to embellish the structural

grid. A subtle draftsmanship, which has the richness of old miniatures but does not become calligraphic and illustrative, marks out the islands of color with a joyful rhythm and presents stupendous glimpses of reality (note the vegetation in the foreground), in an immediate and painstaking representation that does not curb the sense of poetic abandon. As in a converging side-scene, the landscape becomes an essential element of the story and looses into the sky a quiver of light that ignites Christ's body, looking almost as if it is made of alabaster, and organizes the colors: inlays of red, spots of yellow, breaths of green, and expanses of turquoise are disposed in a range of tones that subordinates the form, smoothes out the unevenness, and melts away the masses, creating the work's first level of enchantment: a jubilant gamut of colors, rich in modulations, made up of often discordant tones, but with a skillful orchestration that takes the rules of counterpoint into account, so that the picture assumes the magical appearance of a marvelous tapestry.
(A. Rizzi, in *Capolavori d'arte in Friuli*, 1977)

The miraculous event [the *Healing of a Madman*, Plate 12], observed from the foreground by a group of Venetian patricians, members of the guild and companions of the Calza, goes almost unnoticed in the end, overshadowed by the kaleidoscopic representation of Venice itself. The scene is set at one of the nerve points of the city and at a time very close to the date of Jacopo de' Barbari's plan. The bridge is still the wooden one, built in 1458, with a movable section in the middle to allow the passage of boats, that was to collapse in 1524 and be replaced by the existing stone structure. On the left can be seen the sign of the Albergo dello Storione and the loggia, a meeting place for visitors to the market. On the right we can recognize the Fondaco dei Tedeschi, destroyed in the fire of 1505, Ca' da Mostro with its ground-floor portico that is still standing, the campanile of San Giovanni Crisostomo, and that of Santi Apostoli, reconstructed in 1672. The comparison with the painstaking and analytical realism of the other canvases makes [Carpaccio's] feeling for color and extemporaneous narrative skill stand out even more.
(G. Nepi Sciré, F. Valcanover, *Gallerie dell'Accademia di Venezia*, 1985)

His contemporaries would not have understood the role that Carpaccio has assumed in modern eyes, for in his own day Vittore Carpaccio was not considered to be in the front rank of Venetian painters. The sources mention him only rarely and it seems that he received commissions in his own right from just a few minor guilds, while in the Doge's Palace and the Scuola Grande di San Giovanni Evangelista he had always been overshadowed by the Bellini family. Owing to the settings for which Carpaccio's works were commissioned, not only were the subjects determined in advance but even the shape of the pictures themselves, a low and broad rectangle. It was difficult to fill such large areas with the figures of the protagonists alone, and in any case it was not these, but the whole of the surroundings that stimulated the painter's imagination. At that time the Venetian painting of "historical scenes" comprised a fairly narrow spectrum of emotions: the psychological equivalents of the "andante," "adagio," and "largo." Carpaccio fully shared this conception, and so even his most dramatic scenes, such as the martyrdom of Saint Ursula or the struggle between Saint George and the dragon, have a ceremonial character. Only rarely do the figures have an individual physiognomy. Their attitudes, expressions, and gestures correspond to particular roles: the serious and mature man, the charming young girl of a good family, the handsome adolescent prince. The action, which has a ritual character and is devoid of dramatic developments, is not motivated or explained by the nature of the protagonists. Carpaccio's human beings live passive lives. Whatever happens, their gestures and expressions remain muted, as if frozen by an enchantment. Carpaccio's painting, however gaily colored it may be, is not so serene and lighthearted as has often been claimed.
(N. Huse, W. Wolters, *Venezia. L'arte del Rinascimento*, 1986)

In his two extraordinary "meditations on the dead Christ," Carpaccio invents a space of bones and stones. This quest for hardness and severity could be seen as a sort of rejection in advance of the direction that the young Giorgione was preparing to take.

It is, almost, the last protest of the sharp line and of plastic edges, now condemned to obsolescence by the imminent fusion of the soft style of Perugia, the melted "tone" of Giovanni Bellini, and the *sfumato* of Leonardo.
(A. Chastel, *La grande officina. Arte italiana 1460- 1500*, 1966)

Carpaccio's Saint Ursula cycle, as the first canvas in the series shows, clearly belongs to the same tradition [as the Saint John the Evangelist cycle by Gentile Bellini, Carpaccio, and others], which was by now well established.
His mastery of the illusion of perspective is quite evident throughout—in the extraordinary column in the foreground, for example, or in the little open gate, which seems to penetrate the observer's own space—but the composition of the figures as if in a frieze and the use of color help to create an effect that is above all decorative.
At the same time, the Saint Ursula cycle differs from that of Saint John the Evangelist in the peculiar air of poetic fantasy that pervades it. This is due in part to the differences in the subjects: while the miracles of the True Cross had taken place in his own country and in the recent past, the virgin Princess Ursula had lived in a far-off time and place: and so, while the world portrayed in the *Arrival of the Ambassadors* vividly evokes the city admired by Philippe de Commynes in 1494, it is clear that the painter was also attempting to render his buildings, landscapes, seascapes even more splendid and fabulous than the real Venice. Carpaccio was, in any case, endowed with far greater poetic imagination than the drier and more realistic Gentile Bellini, as is also apparent from his greater sensitivity to the expressive quality of light. In this sense the *Saint Ursula's Dream* is much closer to the spirit of Antonello and Giovanni Bellini than to Gentile, in the beam of light that accompanies the appearance of the angel on the threshold, magically transfiguring the saint's bedroom, and its details seen with the lucid eyes of the Flemish painters.
(P. Humfrey, "La pittura a Venezia nel secondo Quattrocento," in *La pittura in Italia. Il Quattrocento*, 1987)

The presence of music in Carpaccio's large canvases (themselves comparable, in their destination and function, to ceremonial elements) is an area of analysis that deserves further attention. In some of them it is clearly apparent that the sound of music fills the painting, merging with the luministic and chromatic effects that circulate in the atmosphere. Here the chosen hour seems to be that of late afternoon [the reference is to the first canvas, in the chronological sequence of the scenes, in the Saint Ursula cycle], whose golden light kindles the colors and diffuses them, riding on the wave of a synesthesia that assimilates the breath of the wind to the subtle stream of notes. The music rises above the silence of the waiting crowd: in the interval between one chord and the next, one seems to hear the voice of the man reading the message beneath the shrine, creating a counterpoint of sound between the two poles within which the action unfolds. Elsewhere, in the other canvases, the clarions of the musicians will be given the task of spreading the silvery notes that salute the departure of the betrothed couple from the terraces of the royal palace by the sea, or that greet their arrival in Rome from the bastions of Castel Sant'Angelo. Just as it will be the blare of the bugler galloping with his cavalry that gives the signal for the massacre of the pilgrims. And the thread of musical harmony will be woven into other pictures by the artist, from the fanfare of "piercing" trumpets that celebrates the baptism of the Selenites in the Schiavoni cycle to the shepherd's pipe that wafts its melody through the desolate landscape of the *Lament over the Dead Christ* in Berlin.
(L. Zorzi, *Carpaccio e la rappresentazione di Sant'Orsola*, 1988)

His surviving graphic work is richer than that of any other 16th-century painter from Veneto, and so it is possible to study some aspects of the practice of drawing in greater detail, finding support, among other things, for the hypotheses put forward on Giovanni Bellini. In fact, the reconstruction of the method of working used in Carpaccio's workshop confirms and adds elements to the thesis that in Gentile's one, around 1500, a process was carefully developed that entailed the use of different types and techniques of drawing at different stages of the work.
It was Carpaccio's practice to use different degrees of compositional drawing to arrive at the finished design, which incorporated a range of "similar" drawings, and then to

move on from the design to the final painting, in which drawn portraits and other studies of heads were integrated.
(F. Ames-Lewis, "Il disegno nella pratica di bottega del Quattrocento," in *La pittura nel Veneto. Il Quattrocento*, 1990)

Many of Carpaccio's paintings are done on board as was traditional, but the artist often used canvas as well, and more so than the majority of his contemporaries; in Venetian painting the use of canvas as a support only became the norm over the course of the 19th century. This practice of Carpaccio's can be seen as the direct consequence of his painting cycles of narrative pictures, a context in which Jacopo and Gentile Bellini had already been using canvas for several decades. But Carpaccio was the first to use it for altarpieces (in the *Apotheosis of Saint Ursula* for instance), and he was a pioneer in the exploitation of its physical properties to new expressive ends. Carpaccio normally used a very thin preparatory layer, which barely disguised the rough fabric; in addition he often used the new medium, oil painting, in a suggestive manner, more reminiscent of the sketch, with frequent daring touches of pure color that anticipated the picturesque style of Giorgione and Titian. Carpaccio did not have the diligence, the methodical expertise of some of his contemporaries, such as Giovanni Bellini and Cima da Conegliano: when he attained his best results his technique had the merit of expressing greater vividness and spontaneity than did theirs; in his less successful moments it can give the impression of a lack of discipline and even of incompetence.
(P. Humfrey, *Carpaccio. Catalogo completo*, 1991).

Essential Bibliography

G. Perocco, *Tutta la pittura del Carpaccio*, Milan 1960.

R. Pallucchini, *I teleri del Carpaccio in San Giorgio degli Schiavoni*, Milan 1961.

J. Lauts, *Carpaccio: Paintings and Drawings*, London 1962.

Vittore Carpaccio, catalogue of the exhibition at the Doge's Palace, Venice 1963.

G. Perocco, *Carpaccio nella Scuola di San Giorgio degli Schiavoni*, Venice 1964.

M. Muraro, *Carpaccio*, Venice 1965.

P. Zampetti, *Vittore Carpaccio*, Venice 1966.

G. Perocco, *L'opera completa del Carpaccio*, Milan 1967.

M. Serres, *Esthétiques sur Carpaccio*, Paris 1975.

M. Muraro, *I disegni di Vittore Carpaccio*, Florence 1977.

V. Sgarbi, *Carpaccio*, Bologna 1979.

L. Zorzi, *Carpaccio e la rappresentazione di Sant'Orsola*, Turin 1987.

P. Humfrey, *Carpaccio. Catalogo completo*, Florence 1991.